To Celeste – a
wonderful Mother on
Mother's Day 2005.
Love, Mom

Gigi Schweikert

I'm a Good Mother

THE Motherhood CLUB
Making a Difference One Kiss at a Time
mc

A Devotional Book for the
not-so-perfect Mom

HOWARD
PUBLISHING CO.

Our purpose at Howard Publishing is to:

- *Increase faith* in the hearts of growing Christians
- *Inspire holiness* in the lives of believers
- *Instill hope* in the hearts of struggling people everywhere

Because He's coming again!

"*I'm a Good Mother*" © 2005 Gigi Schweikert
All rights reserved. Printed in the United States of America
Published by Howard Publishing Co., Inc.
3117 North 7th Street, West Monroe, LA 71291-2227
www.howardpublishing.com

05 06 07 08 09 10 11 12 13 14   10 9 8 7 6 5 4 3 2 1

Edited by Between the Lines
Interior design by LinDee Loveland

Library of Congress Cataloging-in-Publication Data

Schweikert, Gigi, 1962–
    I'm a good mother : affirmations for the not-so-perfect mom / Gigi Schweikert.
        p. cm.
    ISBN: 1-58229-412-7
    1. Mothers—Miscellanea. 2. Motherhood—Miscellanea. 3. Mother and child—Miscellanea. 4. Child rearing—Miscellanea. 5. Affirmations. I. Title.

HQ759.S2919 2005
242'.6431—dc22

                                              2004054106

Scriptures are taken from the HOLY BIBLE, NEW INTERNATIONAL VERSION®. Copyright © 1973, 1978, 1984 by International Bible Society. Used by permission of Zondervan Publishing House. All rights reserved.

to all the good mothers
—especially my mother

Contents

Contents

Contents

Introduction

You are a good mother. Even though you may not always feel like a good mother or act like a good mother—especially at the end of a long day—God has chosen to give you a child. God sees that "good mother" in you even when you can't.

But He didn't just drop that baby on your doorstep promising to check back when he or she is all grown up. No, God is always right beside you—whether you're rocking your child during a sleepless night, standing over his bed when he's sick, or watching her score the winning goal on the soccer field.

As you read through this book of daily devotions, affirm the good mother you are by putting a star on the chapters in which you already excel. Then build on your successes by setting goals for the Today activities. (Right now your biggest goal may be fitting a shower into your day.) One day at a time, incorporate activities like dreaming with your child, reading with your child, or singing with your child. Little changes make big differences.

Remember how blessed you are. God chose you to raise your beautiful child. He has placed within you what you need to be a capable mother. He knows you'll make some mistakes, but He also knows you can be a good mother.

As a mother comforts her child,
So will I comfort you.

ISAIAH 66:13

7

"I am the most important influence in my child's life and her lifelong teacher."

Being a mom can be overwhelming at times. I often question whether I'm doing what's right—giving my child the love, attention, and discipline he needs to be successful in school and in life. I need to remember how blessed I am and that God chose me to raise this beautiful child because He knows I'm capable. He knows I'll make some mistakes, but He also knows I will be a good mother.

Today

I will be a
confident mother
and thank God
for the opportunity
to raise my child.

Dear Lord, help me to be a good mother. Fill my heart with confidence and the understanding that You trust me to care for and teach this beautiful child.

Train a child in the way he should go,
and when he is old
he will not turn from it.
PROVERBS 22:6

**"I spend time
with my child
so I may talk to him
and teach him."**

Often I'm so busy managing my home, running errands, and taking my child to activities, I wonder how much time I really spend with him. Yes, I'm always around my child, but are we just rushing from place to place and chore to chore? Did I stop to talk to him and play with him? I don't want to miss these fleeting childhood moments. What would God say is most important? I want to create a garland to grace the head of my child.

Today

I will play with my child.
We will read a book together,
take a walk, or
play a board game.
I will talk with my child
and enjoy his company.

Dear heavenly Father, as I move through the day, help me to slow down and enjoy precious moments with my child. Teach me to be *with* my child, not just around him.

Listen, my son, to your father's instruction and do not forsake your mother's teaching. They will be a garland to grace your head and a chain to adorn your neck.
PROVERBS 1:8–9

"I protect my child emotionally and physically."

As a mother I believe my greatest job is to protect my child. I make my home safe and teach her about fires and feelings, but I can't always keep bad things from happening to her. Sometimes she gets sick or hurt or sad, and I wonder if I've done my job well enough. But God is my child's true protector, and I must put my trust in Him. God didn't cause these hurtful things. But God can help me comfort my child and strengthen her to overcome.

Today

I will comfort my child
in whatever way she needs.
I will love her
and encourage her
to overcome life's troubles.

Dear God, give me the strength and wisdom to comfort
my child in sickness, sadness, and pain. Protect my child
from trouble.

You are my hiding place;
you will protect me from trouble
and surround me with songs of deliverance.
PSALM 32:7

"I am an advocate for my child."

Because my child cannot always speak for himself, I am his voice, his petitioner, his advocate. Sometimes my desire for the world to accept and like my child is so great that I unfairly or aggressively assert on his behalf. But do my efforts really stem from the genuine needs of my child or from my own desire for my child to be first? God understands the all-encompassing love I have for my child, but He expects me to be rational. Good decisions are not made based on feelings alone. God knows what my child needs and how I can help him best.

Today

I will be a
rational advocate for my child.
I will act
based on my child's needs
and not just on my emotions.

Dear Lord, temper my emotions and guide me to make
rational decisions regarding my child's needs.

*Speak up for those
who cannot speak for themselves.*
PROVERBS 31:8

"I set the tone in the interactions with my child."

"Not right now." "As soon as I finish." "In a minute." My child says mommy minutes are much longer than regular minutes, and she's right. It's easy to feel overwhelmed with my to-do list in hand—folding the laundry, cooking dinner, talking on the phone. My anger and frustration come bubbling up when my child wants my attention and I'm trying to finish just one more thing. Imagine if I called God's name and He replied, "Just a minute." Yes, there are times when we all need to be patient and wait, but am I always asking my child to wait? The to-do list grows every day—and so does my child.

Today

When my child tugs
at my knees or calls, "Mommy,"
I will turn to her and acknowledge her.
She may still need to wait,
but I will give her a gentle answer,
knowing that every moment
with her is a gift.

Dear God, thank You for this child. Help me to be slow to anger, as You are. When my child calls out to me and I'm busy with the world, let my anger and frustration melt away.

A gentle answer turns away wrath,
but a harsh word stirs up anger.
PROVERBS 15:1

"I teach my child to be generous."

There are toys and treats, goodies and games. Yet no matter how many of these my child has, there will always be someone who has more—and someone who has less. God has given my family so much. How can I teach my child to be thankful for his blessings and to give to others? I will start with the small. My young child can give a kind word, offer a smile, share a toy, or comfort a friend. And as he grows, so will his generosity. His measure will be great, for no matter what he has, my child can always share his love and his time.

Today

I will encourage my child to give
one of his toys or books to someone in need.
Not a forgotten toy or a torn book
but a belonging he is fond of—one that gives him joy.
With that token
he will give to someone else—
and to himself—the gift of joy.

Dear heavenly Father, thank You for Your many blessings. Help my child and me to share them with others. Let us give freely and with great joy.

Give, and it will be given to you.
A good measure, pressed down, shaken together
and running over, will be poured into your lap.
For with the measure you use,
it will be measured to you.
LUKE 6:38

19

"I make our home a place of peace and comfort for my child."

My child will experience bumps and bruises, bullies and failure. Although I won't always be there to protect him from the world, I can make our home a place of peace. I can spark joy with cookies and laughter, soothe boo-boos with Band-Aids and kisses, and calm fears with warm blankets and soft touches. God wants us to live in peace. I can accept His gift of peace by making our home quiet when the world is loud, by making our home safe when the world is scary, and by making our home peaceful when the world is chaotic. I cannot change the world. But through God's great sacrifice, I have the power to be at peace, especially in our home.

Today

My child and I
won't rush out into the busy world.
We will stay home
and snuggle
and find peace.

Thank You, God, for the peace You've given my child and me. When my child is upset or sad, help me to comfort him—to provide security and peace in our home.

I have told you these things, so that in me you
may have peace. In this world you will have trouble.
But take heart! I have overcome the world.
JOHN 16:33

"I have friends who have children."

Being a mom is definitely rewarding, but at times I feel lonely. I long for adult conversation, someone who understands what it feels like to be a mother. Someone who listens to my concerns without necessarily trying to fix them. Someone who laughs and cries with me. I need friends who are moms like me. By spending time with other adults, I'll see that I'm not the only one who has "mommy moments." I'll have a support system of friends, people to help me up when I fall or feel too tired to go on.

Today

I will ask a new friend
to go with me to the park,
come over for tea,
or just push strollers around the block.

Heavenly Father, You have given me so much. How could I ever feel lonely? Yet You understand my need for friends. Surround me with the support of other mothers. Give me the courage to reach out to a new person, to make a new friend.

If one falls down, his friend can help him up.
But pity the man who falls
and has no one to help him up!
ECCLESIASTES 4:10

"I teach my child right from wrong."

Little ones have so many things to learn: to be kind to others, to tell the truth, to be generous, to work hard, to love God. Every day I teach my child something new and remind him of what he's already learned. Still I wonder, will he be ready for the world? There are so many choices and temptations. Will he do what's right? My child may trip and stumble, but God will not let him fall. God will be holding my child's hand even when I am not.

Today

I will help my child
make the right choices,
and I will trust God
to help my child
when I can't.

Dear heavenly Father, thank You for holding my
child's hand. He knows right from wrong, but there are
many ways to stumble. Please hold his hand extra tight
when he's out in the world and I can't be by his side.

If the LORD delights in a man's way,
he makes his steps firm;
though he stumble,
he will not fall,
for the LORD upholds him with his hand.
PSALM 37:23–24

"I show my child how to live joyfully."

Being a mom can be tiring and frustrating. It's easy to be negative—to view life with pessimism and doubt. Sometimes I focus on the day-to-day chores and the hardships of life, yet there are so many joys before me. God's creation is amazing. No matter how difficult I think the day may be, there's always something or someone to be joyful about. I will marvel at the sound of rain, the warmth of my child's hand, and the joy of being a mother.

Today

My child and I will make a list
of all the good things in our lives.
We'll list family and friends,
good food and warm clothes.
We'll add silly songs,
favorite places,
and good books.

Dear Lord, You have filled my life with such joy. Open my eyes and ears that I may share these blessings with my child.

I have told you this so that my joy may be in you
and that your joy may be complete.
JOHN 15:11

"I see my child's true success in her kindness, compassion, and forgiveness."

How do we define success for our children? Our world values high salaries, impressive titles, and fancy cars. I admit that I hope my child grows up to have all of those things and more. But I also want him to extend his hand to a stranger, to have compassion for a person in pain, and to learn to forgive. Intentionally or not, people will say and do hurtful things to my child. A teacher may criticize. A peer may mock. A bully may intimidate. I don't want my child to be a victim, but I do want him to learn to walk away—to take the high road. To forgive others as God has forgiven him.

Today

I will begin
teaching my child about forgiveness
by asking him to forgive me
when I say an unkind word
or lose my patience.

God, fill my heart with forgiveness so it may run over onto my child. Please help me to grow kindness, compassion, and forgiveness in my child.

Be kind and compassionate to one another,
forgiving each other,
just as in Christ God forgave you.
EPHESIANS 4:32

66"I discipline my child."99

Little ones can be so cute, even when they're naughty. But toddler no's grow into teenage no's and more if left uncorrected. It's hard to put limits on my child's behavior or correct him when he does wrong. I can't bear to see him cry when I punish him, and sometimes I'm just too tired to bother. God guides and corrects us with a loving, gentle hand, and that's the best way to discipline my own child. Being a mom takes more than handing out ice cream and kisses. I need the strength and determination to love my child enough to show him how to act. Because if I don't correct him in a loving way, the world will do it harshly.

Today

I will correct my child
if he's misbehaving
and guide him
to do what is right.

Dear God, thank You for trusting me to be a mother. Give me the wisdom and strength to consistently discipline my child with love and gentleness.

No discipline seems pleasant at the time, but painful.
Later on, however, it produces
a harvest of righteousness and peace
for those who have been trained by it.
HEBREWS 12:11

"I rest, and my child rests."

I have never known a job as difficult as that of mother. At times my mind is weary and my body aches. When I feel I cannot possibly read one more book to my child or prepare another meal for my family, God gives me strength.

But even God rested. Each day I will take time to rest and make my child rest too. Children are full of curiosity and energy. Without my gentle guidance, my child will not know to rest and refresh her body so she can continue her adventure of growing up. I will create a daily routine for my child that balances quiet and noise, play and rest. And when my child is resting, I will ignore the chores around me, and I will rest too.

Today

I will nap
when my child naps.
If I cannot actually sleep,
I will lie down
and close my eyes.

Dear heavenly Father, thank You for giving me the strength to be a mother. Place Your peaceful hand upon me, reassuring me that it is good to rest. Clear my mind of all the work of the day, and help me to refresh my body.

By the seventh day God had finished
the work he had been doing;
so on the seventh day he rested from all his work.
GENESIS 2:2

14

"I sing with my child."

No matter how I think my voice sounds, when I sing to my child, it's a beautiful sound. I will sing children's songs and old hymns. I'll sing the songs my mother sang to me. And if I can't remember those songs—or perhaps there weren't any—I will fill my child's memory with songs for her to sing to her children. When my child places her hands on my cheeks and says, "Sing, Mommy," I will sing. And when God looks down upon us, a mother holding her child as they make a joyful noise unto the Lord, may it be a sight to make Him sing.

Today

My child and I
will make up silly songs
about putting away the groceries,
cleaning up the toys,
or finding worms in the backyard.
Tonight I will hold my child
and sing a lullaby.

God, thank You for giving us the gift of music. Help me to share the joy of singing with my child.

Shout for joy to the LORD,
all the earth,
burst into jubilant song with music.
PSALM 98:4

"I guide our family to live as one."

There's no place like home. The familiar sounds and smells, the memories and traditions. What a perfect design God has made in a family—people who love each other, depend on one another, and have common goals. He has given us families so we won't be lonely. During the day my children go off in many directions, yet I take comfort in knowing that as the day draws to a close, we'll all come together again as one—as a family. My most peaceful moment occurs at night, when I touch my sleeping child and remember that a loving home is a place where the family lives as one. My child will know what it means to live as a family. He will never be lonely.

Today

I will plan a
family night with my child.
We will watch a movie
or play a game
or just chat and
enjoy being together.

Thank You, God, for my beautiful family. No matter how far away we are from one another, we can always go home in our hearts because good memories are there— and so are You.

God sets the lonely in families.
PSALM 68:6

"I listen to my child."

My child calls, "Mommy," so many times a day that it's easy to tune her out—to drift off to my own thoughts and concerns. So young, she's eager to share her thoughts now. Will she still confide in me when she's older? Will she trust me to listen to her then?

How many times a day does someone call God's name? Unlike me, He's always eager to hear our calls and patient to listen to our requests. I remember how I felt the first time my child said, "Mama"—so excited, so proud, so pleased. I can't always give my child my complete attention, but I can respond to her and encourage her to talk to me. I will listen to my child.

Today

I will listen to my child
when she calls me,
and I will respond
like it's the first time
she has ever said, "Mama."

God, I realize that as my child grows older and more independent, she will call upon me less. May she always know she can talk to me about anything, and I will listen.

In my distress I called to the LORD;
I called out to my God.
From his temple he heard my voice;
my cry came to his ears.
2 SAMUEL 22:7

"I appreciate my child's individuality."

My child, like a perfectly formed snowflake, is unique. He may look like me at times or even behave in ways I do, but he is an individual, special and like no other. He is just as God has made him.

I try so often to make him what I want him to be. I swim hard against the tide of his life, trying to calm his waves and shape him so all the world will respect and accept him. Yet as he tests the limits of himself and the world, the best way I can help my child is to recognize his skills and talents, build on his successes, and guide him with a firm but gentle hand. He may never be what I want him to be, but he will always be what God intended.

Today

I will look at my child
in a whole new way.
I will accept him
for who he is.

God, thank You for creating every child as an individual. Open my eyes so I can see my child as You do and appreciate him just as he is. Please give me the courage and patience to help him become the adult You want him to be.

My frame was not hidden from you
when I was made in the secret place.
When I was woven together in the depths of the earth,
your eyes saw my unformed body.
PSALM 139:15–16

18

"I cry."

My face was wet with tears when my child first came into my arms. I know that when he's grown, my child will go out into the world and my face again will be wet with tears. I will cry because I can still smell the soft hair of a little boy playing hard; feel the sticky, chubby hands of a toddler; and hear the sweet coos of a baby marveling at the sound of his own voice.

God understands my tears. He knows I will cry when my windows are clean of peanut-butter fingerprints, my kitchen floor quieted of squeaky sneakers, and my laundry no longer a pile. I will cry because my heart is full of the love and memories of being a mom.

And only God can wipe away mommy tears.

Today

I may cry
because of the frustration
and exhaustion
of being a mom.
In the future I will cry
because I miss those very things.

Lord God, You have blessed me as a mother. Soothe my heart when I am weary or frazzled. Let me know that it's all right to cry.

*The Sovereign LORD will wipe away
the tears from all faces.*
ISAIAH 25:8

"I laugh."

I take my job as a mom seriously. I want things to work out just as I imagine—the way mothers look and act on the pages of magazines and in movies. Sometimes when I watch a movie, it feels like those families have more fun, more laughter, more life than mine. It isn't true. It's just that their movie lives are set to music. The orchestration enhances their experience, and because I'm on the outside looking in, it just seems better. If I put my life on the big screen, complete with theme music, I'd see that it too is lively, fun, and full of laughter.

God is directing the movie of my life. All I have to do is live it with love, dignity, and laughter. There are little things to smile about even in the greatest of difficulties. It's all in how I look at the picture.

Today

I will laugh.
I'll laugh at the funny things
my child says,
in conversations with my friends,
and at the silly mistakes I make.
I won't take life so seriously.

God, create in my mind a different picture—the movie of my life, set to music and full of laughter.

She is clothed with strength and dignity;
she can laugh at the days to come.
PROVERBS 31:25

"I do not feel guilty."

Actually, I feel guilty a lot. Why didn't I hold and comfort my child when she was upset instead of yelling at her? When my child came to me with a problem, why did I judge her instead of just listening and trying to help her?

God knows I'm trying to make the right decisions, but so often I fall short of the goal. Every night I ask God, "Was I a good mother today?" He answers, "What do you think?" And I'm not always sure.

I spend too much energy feeling guilty about what I did wrong instead of concentrating on what I did and can do right. I shouldn't. Once God wipes away a failure, it's gone for good. I'm not always the best mom I can be, but He knows I'm always trying.

Today

I will name three things
I did well as a mom.
I will let go of the things
I could have done better.

Heavenly Father, help me to focus on the many wonderful things I do as a mother. As I confess my failures and shortcomings to You, let them melt away and be forgotten.

As far as the east is from the west,
so far has he removed our transgressions from us.
PSALM 103:12

"I spend time outside each day with my child."

Sometimes the only moment my child and I share outside is when we rush from the house to the car. As she stops to stuff acorns in her pocket or explore the merits of each rock in our driveway, I say, "Hurry up. Please put that down" because we're off to learn and grow somewhere else, indoors, in a classroom with other children. I forget how much there is for my child to learn outside, right in our own backyard. She needs time to run and roll, explore and examine. Maybe it's easier to stay inside and not get dirty, but God has created a beautiful world for us to enjoy, and I want to share it with my child.

Today

Even if it rains or snows,
my child and I
will spend time outside.
We will stomp in puddles
or catch snowflakes on our tongues
or bask in the warm sun.
We will breathe in the beauty around us.

Dear God, the trees, the sky, the landscape are gifts to enjoy. Help me to make going outside each day with my child a priority.

*He said to me, "Get up and go out to the plain,
and there I will speak to you."*
EZEKIEL 3:22

"My behavior is the greatest influence on my child's behavior."

I realize that my child is watching everything I do and say. I've seen him imitate me when he pretends to talk on the phone or care for the baby. Even before he could talk, my child could shake his finger or put his hand on his hip just like I do.

I have many things to tell my child about the world. I tell him not to cross the street unless the light is red—then I cross on green if no cars are coming. I tell him not to lie, then say, "She's not here" to the person on the phone asking for me.

"Do as I say, not as I do" won't work. If I want my child to act a certain way, I'll have to act that way too.

Today

I will remember
that my child is watching me.
I will say please
and thank you,
and I'll treat friends,
family, and strangers
with kindness and respect.

Dear heavenly Father, my child looks to me for guidance. Help me say the right things, but more importantly, help me to be like Christ.

*Follow my example,
as I follow the example of Christ.*
1 CORINTHIANS 11:1

"I teach my child to enjoy his work and to do his best."

I imagine telling friends and family of my child's many successes when he grows up: He's a sports star and holds a world record. He's a businessman and makes lots of money. He's a doctor and saves lives.

Maybe my child will be one of those things. But it's more important that he be happy in his work. I feel myself pushing for what I want him to be, but that's not necessarily what God sees for him or even what my child wants. I will let my child experience many kinds of worthwhile work. I'll give him choices so he can practice his talents and skills. I want him to be happy in his work, for that is a gift from God.

Today

I will guide my child
as he shows interest in a particular topic,
whatever that is.
If he likes rocks,
we will collect rocks big and small.
We'll visit a mine and read books
about rocks at the library.
I will help my child find joy in his tasks.

∽

Dear God, I want to be accepting and supportive of my child's interests and work. Help me to let go of my plans and give him the freedom and encouragement to follow his own path.

To accept his lot and be happy in his work—
this is a gift of God.
ECCLESIASTES 5:19

"I am consistent."

As I depend upon God, so my child depends upon me. I don't gather a candle and matches for fear the sun may not shine tomorrow. I know the morning light will come as it always does, and in that sameness I feel secure. My child looks to me for consistency to know that after lunch will come a nap. After hurt, a kiss. After play, a bath. Simple routine—knowing what to expect—makes my child feel secure. When she looks to me for a smile after a job well done or hesitates after touching something she shouldn't, waiting for correction, she is depending on my consistency to make her world feel stable.

Today

I will follow a simple routine.
I will be full of smiles
and love for my child,
and I also will say no
when it needs to be said.

∞

Dear Lord, thank You for Your sameness—for Your love that endures forever. Give me the consistency I need to help my child feel safe and secure.

Give thanks to the LORD,
for he is good.
His love endures forever.
PSALM 136:1

55

"I work to understand and appreciate my child's perspective."

What must it be like to never be able to reach the things you want? To have no choice but to eat what you're given? As a mom, I make countless choices every day. My child has few choices.

He must wait without recourse when I say, "Just a minute" and proceed to chat with a friend for fifteen. My child cries when the shopping carries over to lunch. He's tired and hungry and can do nothing to relieve either feeling.

Sometimes it seems appealing to only have the cares of a child. But do I really understand what that's like?

Today

When my child is upset,
I will try to understand
how he really feels
and why.

God, help me to see the world through the eyes of my child—to understand and appreciate his perspective.

"My thoughts are not your thoughts,
neither are your ways my ways,"
declares the LORD.
ISAIAH 55:8

"I demand mutual respect between my child and me."

Teaching my child to be respectful is a tough job. Demanding mutual respect between my child and me is even tougher.

Respect isn't being afraid or having no voice or obeying without question. It's being willing to listen to and value a person's opinions even if you don't agree. Yes, I am the adult, and I make the final decisions regarding my child's life. But I will listen to her ideas, encourage her to share her perspective, and increasingly let her make some of her own decisions. Through it all I will teach—and give—my child respect.

Today

I will show my child
respect by listening
to her thoughts
and ideas.

Dear Lord, as a mom I'm responsible for decisions regarding my child. But open my ears and my heart to value her ideas. I will respect her, and in turn she will respect me—not just because I demand it, but because she feels it.

Show proper respect to everyone.
1 PETER 2:17

"I don't worry what others think of me."

I often glance at the women I see around me and try to imagine what their lives are like. Somehow I think they have obedient children in pressed, white clothes; sparkling kitchens with homemade desserts; and happy, perfect lives. And I wonder, why can't I be like that? I worry what they think of me. Will people like me? Will they think my kids are cute and well behaved? Will they think I'm a good mother?

Ultimately, it doesn't matter what others think. I am accountable only to God. I know I'll make mistakes, but I'll keep trying. God knows I'm doing my best. And that's what counts.

Today

I will not
compare myself with others
or wonder what they think of me.

God, thank You for loving me unconditionally, like I love my child. Help me not to worry about what others think of me.

Be imitators of God, therefore,
as dearly loved children
and live a life of love.
EPHESIANS 5:1–2

"I am pleased with my efforts to meet the many demands in our family's life."

It's so easy to pick at the threads of life—seeing only the pulls and frays, never appreciating the beautiful tapestry. I work hard for my child and my family. Yet often I'm critical of these efforts—always feeling I should do more, give a little extra. I never pull the quilt of my work around me and feel the warmth of all I've given. But my child knows. He snuggles into my hugs, responds to my touch, reciprocates my love. My child, in his own sweet way, calls me blessed.

Today

I will write down
three good things I did as a mother—
things like bringing
warm clothes straight from the dryer,
bandaging a hurt that really only needed a kiss,
or extra hugs for no reason at all.
I will appreciate my efforts.

Oh, God. Why am I never satisfied? Help me to feel good about the work I've done and to realize that my child is blessed by my efforts.

Her children arise
and call her blessed.
PROVERBS 31:28

"I eat dinner with my child."

Rush, rush, rush. It seems like I never have time to sit down and eat, so I stand—nibbling here and gulping there. I scarf down the unwanted crusts of peanut-butter-and-jelly sandwiches and slightly gummed cookies picked clean of the chocolate chips. I watch my child eat as I scurry about the kitchen or chat on the phone.

Dinner should be not just a time to nourish my body but also a time to sit down and connect with my child. I make time for social dinners and work dinners, but I need to take time for family dinners. Whether I'm serving pasta or cold cereal, every time I eat with my child, I'll think of it as a family feast—a celebration.

Today

I will sit down
and have dinner
with my child.

Dear Lord, thank You for the food you have given us
and for this mealtime we share as a family.

His sons used to take turns holding feasts in their homes,
and they would invite their three sisters
to eat and drink with them.

JOB 1:4

"I develop family traditions with my child."

Home is a feeling. It's the sound of the people who live there, working, laughing, and sometimes crying. Home is the memories you hold in your heart. I want my child to hold precious memories, to have traditions he can share with his child and his children's children.

Traditions can be festive, like tree lightings and holiday feasts, or simple, like marking on the doorframe how much my child has grown. We'll make special memories together of childhood and of family. And when my child shares them with his own children, wherever life may take him, he will feel at home.

Today

I will begin a tradition with my child.
We will count the steps leading to our front door or
take a photograph every year at the same time,
in the same place,
or go for a walk
after each holiday meal.

Heavenly Father, help me to appreciate the beauty of the simple traditions we make in our lives. Remind me that cherished childhood memories are not made of expensive gifts or fancy parties but of simple acts repeated with love and passed down through generations.

Tell it to your children,
and let your children tell it to their children,
and their children to the next generation.

JOEL 1:3

"I dream with my child."

I remember lying on my back as a child and watching the sky—naming the shapes of clouds floating by, thinking about life—just daydreaming. Simple thoughts and conversations can spark the imagination, plant a seed of curiosity, or give birth to a dream. Every job well done, every great accomplishment begins with a thought—with a dream.

God has given us so many opportunities. He has given us the freedom to make choices, to follow a path made especially for each of us. I want my child to dream, to imagine all the possibilities God has for her.

Today

I will sit with my child
and watch the water rush over the rocks in a stream
or the clouds float by
or people hurrying along the avenue.
My child and I will talk
and daydream.

God, please slow my pace. Give me time with my child
to watch the world unfold, to dream about our place in
Your creation, and to discover Your good plans for us.

"I know the plans I have for you," declares the LORD,
"plans to prosper you and not to harm you,
plans to give you hope and a future."
JEREMIAH 29:11

"I read to my child."

Nothing is more precious than a mother reading to her child. When I read to my child, she can feel the warmth of my body as she sits on my lap; hear the sweetness of my voice; know the comfort of time shared. And she learns. She learns about literature, science, art, and fun.

Even when my child can read on her own, I will still read to her. I will read *Treasure Island, Huckleberry Finn,* and the Bible. And when I'm old and my eyes are tired, my child will read to me. I will feel the warmth of her body as she sits next to me; savor the sweetness of her voice; and cherish the comfort of all the times we've shared.

Today

I will read to my child,
whether she's an infant,
a toddler, or a teenager.
I will draw her close
and spend time reading together.

∞

Dear Lord, remind me to read to my child every day. Let me fill her with a love of literature, learning, and Your Word.

"Do you understand what you are reading?" Philip asked.
"How can I," he said,
"unless someone explains it to me?"
ACTS 8:30–31

"I accept my child as she is."

When God lays the gift of a child in a mother's arms, she sees a perfect baby. My child doesn't have to have ten fingers and ten toes to be amazing in my eyes. But the world doesn't always see through my eyes. Others may judge my child more harshly. They may notice that he's small for his age, or that he sits in a wheelchair, or that he doesn't talk even though he's eight.

Sometimes I wonder why my child is not like other children. Did I do something wrong? Is God punishing me? No! God *chose* me. He was looking for a very special mother—one who would see the perfection in this child, because He knew the world could not.

Today

I will accept my child
for who she is.
I will be proud and not ashamed.
I will see the perfection God
has placed in my child
that the rest of the world misses.

Dear heavenly Father, sometimes I question why You brought this child to me. Reassure me. Please give me strength when I'm exhausted, and perseverance when I'm discouraged.

*Accept one another, then, just as Christ accepted you,
in order to bring praise to God.*
ROMANS 15:7

"I ask my child for forgiveness."

I love my child, but sometimes I'm selfish, frustrated, and exhausted. I dream about the days before my child, when I could read and sleep and shower. I tire of cleaning dishes, washing clothes, playing silly games, and having my child constantly at my side. I say unkind things. I'm impatient. In anger I yell, "What's the matter with you? What were you thinking?" I forget my child is still learning and growing.

I will ask my child for forgiveness. I will show her that even mommies make wrong choices and say the wrong things. I will teach her forgiveness by forgiving her shortcomings—and confessing my own.

Today

When I raise my voice
unnecessarily,
I will tell my child I'm sorry.
I will ask her
to forgive me.

God, help me to be a good example for my child.
Release me of my pride so I may ask forgiveness of those
around me, especially my child.

Bear with each other and forgive
whatever grievances you may have against one another.
Forgive as the Lord forgave you.
COLOSSIANS 3:13

"I share decision making when appropriate."

While my child is small, I must make almost all of his decisions for him. Without my intervention, he would eat cookies all day, never nap, and take baths only in puddles. So I guide my child. I map out his day.

When he's older, I will still want to guide him—to spare him mistakes and consequences. But gradually I must let him make his own decisions. I'll talk with him about his choices, but I'll let him make some mistakes so he can learn better decision-making skills for next time.

My child will make wrong turns and wind up on difficult paths. But I will give him the tools he needs to chart his own course and teach him to look to God to guide his steps.

Today

I will offer my child choices.
I will let him decide
when he will do his homework.
If he doesn't complete the assignment,
I will let him experience the consequences.

Dear Lord, it's so hard to let my child make his own decisions. I want to be his protector, his guide. Help me to let go and realize that You are his protector, and You will guide him through life.

In his heart a man plans his course,
but the LORD determines his steps.
PROVERBS 16:9

"I expect excellence, not perfection, from my child."

It's hard to let my child dress herself or make her bed. Her clothes don't always match, and her bedsheet hangs down from under the comforter. Why can't I let my child's work be different from the way I would do it?

Her hands are small, but her determination is big. I don't want to criticize or redo the work my child completes. I don't want her to stop trying. My child has her own way of doing things, and I want to focus on those rather than getting stuck on my method. I expect excellence from my child, not perfection. Because my way isn't perfect either. The only perfect way is God's—and I'm not sure He cares about the sheet.

Today

I will not stand
in the way
of my child's determination.
I will realize there's more than one way
to gets things done.

Lord, You have given me a child with wonderful skills and talents. Don't let me stand in the way of my child doing her best.

Do not embitter your children,
or they will become discouraged.
COLOSSIANS 3:21

"I celebrate my child's best efforts and successes."

When my child was a baby, he looked up at me, searching for my smile anytime he pulled up or clapped his hands. I responded with smiles and claps of my own. His every move was a triumph.

Now that he's older, have I forgotten how to encourage his efforts, to celebrate his successes? Controlling his anger, helping a friend, and playing soccer even though he knows he's not the best on the team are acts worthy of my attention.

My child shouldn't need validation for everything he does, and in time just knowing he has worked with all his heart will be enough reward for him. But I'll keep cheering, because that's what good mothers do.

Today

I will notice the little things
my child does well and acknowledge them,
whether it's cleaning up
without being asked,
sharing with a friend,
or trying to control his emotions.

Lord, my child continues to search for my approval. Help me to notice his efforts each day and to celebrate them.

Whatever you do,
work at it with all your heart,
as working for the Lord, not for men.
COLOSSIANS 3:23

❝I am organized.❞

I try to be organized. It's not my intention to forget the class cupcakes or to dress my child in purple on orange day. Sometimes it just seems easiest to live in a kind of chaos, tackling projects as they come, ignoring what I miss, and using motherhood as an excuse. But there's nothing chaotic about God's world. And no one, especially my child, benefits from my not having some organization. That doesn't mean I have to have a spotless home, closets with labels for where things go, or a calendar with every activity marked. Being organized is really about knowing my responsibilities, prioritizing the work to be done, and using time as a gift. There's no right way to get organized, but the lack of it will keep me from caring for my child, my home, and myself as well as I could.

Today

I will complete a project
I've been avoiding.
I'll clean out a drawer,
clear papers off my kitchen counter,
or put away the clothes on my bed.

Lord, I admit I could be more organized. Help me to know the peace of order in my days and to honor You by honoring my commitments.

*God is not a God of disorder
but of peace.*
1 CORINTHIANS 14:33

"I pray for my child every day."

My day is spent caring for my child making sure her tummy is full, her clothes are warm and clean, her days are pleasant, and her life is good. That's hard work, but I am not caring for her alone. God is caring for both of us.

I usually find myself asking for His help only when I'm desperate or have exhausted all my motherly ways. I forget that I can ask God to help me with the little things—to quiet my child when she's upset, to help her feel secure in my absence, to fill her world with good things. God will help me give my child what she needs. All I have to do is ask.

Today

I will pray for my child
when her day begins and
at night when she goes to sleep.
And soon I will learn to pray before all else.

Dear heavenly Father, remind me to lean on You. Help me to remember that I'm not raising this child alone. I have You.

I call on you, O God,
for you will answer me;
give ear to me and hear my prayer.
PSALM 17:6

"I am confident."

Am I spending enough time with my child? Do I discipline him enough? Am I involved with his school? Will he find his way in the world without me by his side?

Why do I worry so much about my child and the decisions I make concerning him? The simple answer is, because I love him.

Life offers so many choices it can feel overwhelming. But I must be confident, knowing that I'm doing my best and that God is with me. Confident doesn't mean always knowing and never doubting. Confidence is making a decision, assessing how things go along the way, and making changes as needed. God has confidence in me, now I must have confidence in myself.

Today

I will consider
all the possibilities
regarding my child's care,
and then I will make a decision
with confidence.
I won't doubt my actions.

Dear Lord, give me the confidence to care for my child the best way I can. Wash away my doubt, and fill me with Your assurance.

Do not throw away your confidence;
it will be richly rewarded.
HEBREWS 10:35

"I play with my child."

"You're always too busy to play," my child says. What am I doing that's more important than playing with her, than being with my child? The laundry, the dishes, paperwork? I have to do those things, yes. But I don't want to miss the magic of life because I'm too occupied with the business of living. You're never too old to play, to enjoy games, to laugh, to have fun. Most of us have just forgotten how. While my child is young, we will run on the beach, play peek-a-boo and hide-and-seek. When she's older, we'll watch a movie, go skating and shopping. All too soon I'll call my child, and she will be too busy for me. She'll be playing with her own children.

Today

I will stop and play.
I will leave the sink
filled with dishes
and go do something fun
with my child.

God, help me to enjoy the moments You've given me
this day by taking time to play with my child.

The city streets will be filled
with boys and girls
playing there.
ZECHARIAH 8:5

"I watch my child sleep."

There is no greater calm than a sleeping child. The world should move to the rhythm of a sleeping baby's breaths.

Sometimes at the end of a busy day, when my child is finally in bed and I've straightened up the house, putting away the odds and ends of our hurried activity, I watch her sleep . . . and wonder . . . How could I ever raise my voice to this innocent one, be impatient with her wonder, dampen her exuberance? When I stand in the presence of my sleeping child, I can feel angels around her . . . in the still of the room, the presence of God.

Today

I will watch my child sleep.
I will listen to her peaceful breathing
and smile at the way her soft hair
has fallen around her face.

Dear God, when I'm irritated and frustrated with my child, bring me to the calmness of her slumber. Put an image of her sleeping face in my mind.

> *I will lie down and sleep in peace,*
> *for you alone, O LORD,*
> *make me dwell in safety.*
> PSALM 4:8

"I encourage my child's creativity."

Play-Doh gets stuck in the carpet. Paint ends up more on my walls and on my child than on the paper. What a mess! Some days I'd rather have my child watch a video or play with blocks or read.

But then I remember the thrill of filling a big, white page with wild color. I imagine God must have felt that way when He created the heavens and the earth, pouring out color where there had been nothing.

My child is filled with creativity. He hasn't been jaded with inhibitions of "I can't draw." My child is full of "I can." I will encourage his creativity by allowing him to get messy and have fun—to create in the image of his Creator.

Today

I will find a place
for my child to get messy,
to have fun,
to be creative.
We'll head to the garage with paints
or drape a cloth over the kitchen table
and create something wonderful.

Dear heavenly Father, I want to foster my child's creativity and his uninhibited attitude that he can do anything. Help me to forget about the mess and concentrate on the making.

*I meditate on all your works
and consider what your hands have done.*
PSALM 143:5

44

"I make our home a place my child and his friends want to be."

When people come over, sometimes I feel inconvenienced or unprepared. It upsets my schedule and my plans. "Dropping by" seems like a thing of the past—and an imposition. It shouldn't.

I will welcome friends and neighbors into my home. My door will always be open, especially to my child's friends. It won't matter whether my house is clean or if I have food to offer. I will offer them the comfort and safety of my home. I will give my time and my friendship. I want my child's friends, from whatever situation they come, to know what it's like to be home. And I want my child to know the joy of sharing his home with others.

Today

I will invite
another child
over to play
with my child.

Heavenly Father, You have asked me to offer hospitality to others. Please help me to be welcoming—comforting in conversation and generous with the food and drink You've so generously given me.

Offer hospitality to one another
without grumbling.
1 PETER 4:9

"I help my child develop confidence."

With a can-do attitude and God's help, the possibilities for my child are endless. I want her to accept the blessings of life without hesitation. I want her to push through the hardships of life with determination.

Confidence isn't pride or arrogance. It's the strength of mind to know that no matter what life has to offer, you can make the most of it—find the silver lining. It's not worrying about what others think and not being anxious about things that may never happen.

I help my child to be confident when I encourage her. I will teach her to always look for the silver lining in life, in herself, and in others.

Today

I will encourage my child
when she says, "I can't."
I will help her break the tasks
into little steps,
and together
we will conquer each one.

Lord, when my child is hesitant, when she thinks she's not capable, when she lacks confidence, extend Your grace and guide her steps so she will not give up.

Encourage one another
and build each other up.
1 THESSALONIANS 5:11

"I set boundaries for my child."

As my child grows, his boundaries expand. My infant was only an arm's reach away. My toddler was always in my sight. My preschooler played in the next room. But he was always testing where he could go and what he could do. So I taught him, putting him back in the circle of my care when he ran out or did something incorrect.

I want my child to explore God's world and to become more independent, but I also want him to be safe and prepared. So I set boundaries. And as my child grows and is confronted with the evils of the world, he will feel the invisible circle I've drawn around him. He will put himself back into that circle of safety.

Today

I will be firm
when my child pushes the boundaries,
when I say, "One Cookie,"
and he wants another.
I will not give in when my child begs
for something at the store.
I will say no
when my child asks to go to a party
without adult supervision.

Dear Lord, as You have set loving boundaries for me, let me draw a circle around my child so that he too will be under Your protection.

Do what is right and good
in the LORD's sight.
DEUTERONOMY 6:18

47

"I pray with my child."

I talk to God throughout my day, yet my child rarely sees or hears me pray because my prayers are silent words of thanksgiving and request. I want my child to have her own personal time of prayer and to develop her own relationship with God. Since my child learns more from my actions than from my words, I will let her hear me and see me pray. I will pray with my child. We will pray before meals and at night before sleep. When an ambulance goes by, when someone is sad, or when someone needs help, I will pray aloud so my child can hear me and learn.

Today

I will pray with my child
before every meal and
thank God for His many blessings.

Lord, don't let me forget to pray with my child, to spend
time sharing the joy of talking with You.

Whatever you ask for in prayer,
believe that you have received it,
and it will be yours.
MARK 11:24

48

"I teach my child not to be afraid."

It's scary when the thunder is loud, when your mother leaves you with a sitter, when you see shadows in your room at night. These are the fears of my child—so simple, so easy to overcome, I think. But my child is so frightened that he calls my name in the night. I go to him, comfort and hold him, reassuring him that there's nothing to fear—that he is safe. Who will comfort my child when he's old and I'm not there to answer his call? God will. I know my child will have doubts and concerns. A nightlight won't always chase away his monsters. So I will teach my child not to be afraid by teaching him to rely on God.

Today

I will tell my child
there's no such thing as a monster,
but I'll still check under his bed
and in his closet
to reassure him.

God, You comfort me when I'm afraid. Please offer Your reassurance through my hands as I comfort my child in times of fear and doubt.

*I am the LORD, your God,
who takes hold of your right hand and says to you,
Do not fear; I will help you.*
ISAIAH 41:13

"I have quiet times each day."

I am rarely still and quiet. Guilt comes over me if I sit down during the middle of the day. I always feel like I should be doing something. Why? I suppose our society has come to value the productive—the doers and accumulators of things. But my child and I need quiet time to think and pray and listen to God. There's nothing wrong with looking out the window or sitting on the porch. It's my responsibility to protect my family's quiet time. I must make it a priority, or the world will take it from us.

Today

I will not answer the telephone
when we're eating.
I will turn off the television
and the radio,
and we will be quiet.

God, I know You have called me to rest. Help me show my child how to appreciate and protect times of quiet reflection.

He said to them,
"Come with me by yourselves to a quiet place."
MARK 6:31

" I volunteer to help at my child's school. "

I realize I can't be involved in everything. Even though I have many jobs, this is the time God has given me to be a mother, to be involved in my child's life. By helping at my child's school, I show him that I'm interested in his life. And he's glad I'm involved, even if he says otherwise.

It's easy to bake cupcakes and go on field trips when my child is young, but how will I stay involved as he grows? I can join the parent-teacher association, attend school-board meetings, go to open house and back-to-school nights. I can ask my child questions about his schoolwork, teachers, and friends. And, of course, no child is really too old for cupcakes.

Today

I will call my child's teacher
and ask how I can help.

God, sometimes it's easier to let others volunteer. I think they have more talent and time. Show me how I can make a difference in my child's education.

Each one should use whatever gift
he has received to serve others,
faithfully administering God's grace
in its various forms.
1 PETER 4:10

51

❝I take care of myself so I can care for my child.❞

My days are filled with giving to others: making meals, running errands, helping friends, being there for my child. But I can't continue to give of myself without putting something back. Taking care of myself enables me to take better care of my child. I need to rest, exercise, and eat well to be healthy. I need time alone to be a better person when I'm with others.

I want to be appreciated, and it feels good to be acknowledged for all I do. But I know that self-worth comes from within—from knowing I'm doing exactly what God wants me to do. And to do what God wants, I must take care of myself.

Today

I will do something for me—
read a book,
take a walk, or
have lunch with a friend.

God, I know I'm worthy because You have trusted me to be a mother. Please help me rejuvenate my body and refill my heart so I can continue giving to my child and to others.

In quietness and trust is your strength.
ISAIAH 30:15

“I control my anger.”

My child dumps my neatly folded laundry on the floor . . . scribbles on the wall with green permanent marker . . . breaks the window with a ball . . . wrecks the car. My first response is anger and frustration. I yell. I hurl questions without waiting for answers. I lose control of my emotions. Yes, my child needs to learn to be more careful—not to do these things. I want her to be safe. But somehow I must use these mistakes and misdeeds to teach her. Crazy, ranting, out-of-control behavior isn't the best way to teach. I will tell my child that I'm angry and why, but I will control my anger. I will use each misstep as an opportunity to teach my child, to tell her the correct thing to do and the consequences of her actions.

Today

When my child behaves
in a way that makes me angry,
I will stop before yelling.
I will gain control.

Why, Lord, do I get angry so easily? Use these times when I teach my child to also help me learn that a quick temper is foolish and not helpful to anyone.

A quick-tempered man does foolish things.
PROVERBS 14:17

"I am content as a mother."

There have been many stages in my life: child, student, newlywed, and now mother. My time is no longer my own. All my decisions and choices revolve around my child. I'm not as free to do what I want when I want. Sometimes I long for sleep-in mornings and spontaneous weekend trips. I mourn career opportunities lost and priorities changed.

But I don't want to wish away the days of motherhood. I remind myself that just because the world's most important job doesn't come with a paycheck doesn't mean it lacks rewards: wet, slurpy kisses . . . gooey little handprints . . . shockingly powerful love. And then I remember that being a mother is exactly what I want to do.

Today

I will look
for the small rewards of mothering—
my child's smile,
outstretched arms seeking my embrace,
and deliciously sloppy kisses.

Dear God, when I'm restless in my role as a mother, help me to be content. Remind me that there's no other job as important as being a mom.

*I have learned to be content
whatever the circumstances.*
PHILIPPIANS 4:11

"I overcome my own fears for my child."

I tell my child, "Don't be afraid. It's all right. Mommy's with you." But I have fears of my own. Being a mother has helped me push past many of them. When I thought I could not possibly handle one more thing, God gave me the strength for seemingly endless hours of labor, sleepless nights, colds and coughs, and emotional exhaustion. I have survived them all.

I've grown and learned in my world of motherhood. As my child grows, she steps farther out into the big world, and I must go with her. To guide her, I must conquer my own fears. As I face with courage the things that frighten me, my child will learn that she can overcome her fears too.

Today

I will take the first step
in conquering one of my fears.
I will name my fear
and visualize myself overcoming it.

Dear heavenly Father, like my child, I am sometimes afraid. Please give me the strength to confront my fears and to persevere through them so they won't keep me from being the best mother I can be.

The Lord is my helper;
I will not be afraid.
HEBREWS 13:6

"I teach my child to be thankful."

I teach my child to say thank you from the time he's a toddler. "Tank ou," he says when I give him a cookie or a toy. "Thanks!" he says for skateboards and school trips. Sometimes I wonder, do I give him too much? My child knows how to say thank you, but is he thankful?

True gratitude is the acknowledgment of a gift—not a present with a big bow but a gift that doesn't fit in a box at all. Thankfulness is appreciating the gifts of love, home, forgiveness, shelter, provision.

It's hard to learn gratitude for something except in its absence. I don't want my child to go without, and with God's help he will lack none of those gifts. But I will do my best to help him be thankful.

Today

I will ask my child
to tell me three things
for which he is thankful.

Dear God, I struggle with the lesson of thankfulness—
even I'm not always aware of how blessed I am. Teach
me to help my child appreciate the gifts in his life.

Give thanks to the LORD, for he is good;
his love endures forever.
PSALM 106:1

"I learn from my child."

I didn't know that a saltine cracker has thirteen holes. I didn't remember the names of the seven continents and four oceans. I forget when to choke up on the bat, and I'm surprised to learn there's more than one way to tie a shoe.

My child is discovering the world and its mysteries with an enthusiasm and excitement that I've lost to years and experience. Her mind is full of curiosity. Her energy is boundless. Her sadness, hurt, and anger fade quickly without resentment. Through motherhood, God is giving me a second childhood—a chance to find what I'd forgotten . . . and to learn what I didn't catch the first time.

Today

I will play alongside my child
and open my eyes
to the miracles
so we can learn together.

Dear Lord, help me remember that I don't need to know all the answers to raise my child; I only need the willingness to learn. Surprise me, God, with Your wondrous world.

Let the wise listen and add to their learning,
and let the discerning get guidance.
PROVERBS 1:5

"I make simple things special for my child."

Every day is a celebration of God's love. Sometimes staying at home and doing the everyday tasks of caring for my child seems unimportant. My days become routine, mundane, ordinary. I forget how precious this time with my child is. I am creating a childhood. What will my grown child's tales of this time be like? She probably won't reminisce about fancy gifts or big events but rather about the little things. There are so many things I can do to make even the simple times special—wake her with a kiss, make letter-shaped pancakes that spell out her name, put juice in a coffee cup and have morning "coffee" together. We'll go on picnics and hikes and sleep overnight in the backyard, and bake cakes for no reason . . . for the best reason of all.

Today

I will make my child's day more special.
I'll put a love note in her lunchbox,
rent a movie for family night,
or serve milk in fancy glasses.

Dear Lord, each day I spend with my child is a special day, a day of celebration. Remind me of the pleasure and blessing of the simple.

A man can do nothing better than to eat and drink
and find satisfaction in his work.
This too, I see, is from the hand of God.
ECCLESIASTES 2:24

58

"I show my child the world."

Getting out of the house can be difficult with a child. Sometimes it's just easier to leave him at home. Alone I can accomplish errands quickly. I don't have to worry about how my child will act in public. Maybe he doesn't behave so well at first; but he'll never learn social skills—or much else—if he's never out in the world.

Oh, there are places and things I don't want my child to see. But the wonders of the world—the amazing things God has made—those I want my child to know. Trips to the post office, the grocery store, and the local park may seem insignificant, but they're a start—a training ground for trips to the Appalachian Mountains . . . the Pacific Ocean . . . for his grand journey into the world.

Today

I'll take my child
to the library or
a concert in the park
or the town fair.

God, I often hesitate to take my child out into this wonderful world You have created for us. Please remind me that learning comes not only from books but also from experience.

Call to me and I will answer you and
tell you great and unsearchable things
you do not know.
JEREMIAH 33:3

"I am the best mother I can be."

Every night as my child drifts off to sleep, I vow I will be an even better mom tomorrow. Most evenings I think about the things I should have done better—I should have been more patient, lowered my voice, spent more time with my child. Why do I look past my best efforts—the love in my heart, my hopes for my child, my desire to be the best I can be?

There's no best-mother award, no financial bonus for the most kisses. But there are *I love you*'s from my child, lively dinners with my family, and the privilege of striving every day to be the best mother I can be.

Today

I will realize
that there are ways for me
to be an even better mother,
but I will also acknowledge
the things I do well.

Heavenly Father, may I wake each morning with the excitement of a new day, with the desire and Your help to be the best mom I can be.

Here am I, and the children
the LORD has given me.
ISAIAH 8:18

"I am blessed to be a mother."

I always knew I wanted to be a mother someday, but I never really knew what to expect. I don't think any woman really does. When I was waiting for my child to come, people said, "A child will change your life." They were right. Every day is still a surprise. I still don't know what to expect. So I rely on God to guide me in the adventure of motherhood. And what an adventure it is. Why did He choose me to raise this child? Did He know my heart was full of love? Did He know I was stronger than I thought? Whatever God knew, I'm so glad He trusted me to rock this child to sleep, to kiss away the pain, to nurture and prepare. He must have known how I would treasure the blessing of my child—of being a mother.

Today

I will give thanks
for being
a mother.

God, You have given me the greatest gift a woman can receive. You have made me a mother. And I am blessed.

When her baby is born she forgets the anguish
because of her joy that a child is born into the world.
JOHN 16:21

THE M♥therhood CLUB™
Making a Difference One Kiss at a Time
mc

... born from a simple idea: *honor Mom for doing the most important job in the world.*

Titles included in **THE M♥therhood CLUB**™:

Prayer Guide: *The Busy Mom's Guide to Prayer*
—*Lisa Whelchel*

Parenting: *Mom-CEO*
—*Teresa Bell Kindred*

There's a Perfect Little Angel in Every Child
—*Gigi Schweikert*

Inspiration: *The Miracle in a Mother's Hug*
—*Helen Burns*

Gift: *Holding the World by the Hand*
—*Gigi Schweikert*

Fiction: *Tight Squeeze*
—*Debbie DiGiovanni*

Devotional: *"I'm a Good Mother*
—*Gigi Schweikert*

"At The Motherhood
Club, you'll find b
to meet all your
mothering needs.
—*Lisa Whelchel*
(From *The Facts o*